# THE SPELL CRAFTER'S COMPENDIUM

Correspondences for witchcraft spells and rituals

By Terri Paajanen

ISBN: 978-0-09916711-3-7


Originally published via Kindle in 2013

# ABOUT THE AUTHOR

Terri has been a practicing witch for more than 20 years and has been involved with Pagan projects such as the online community Covenspace, Little Pagan Acorns kid's printables and even wrote on Paganism & Wicca for About.com many years ago.

Even so, she still often needs a correspondence guide to help her remember all the various magickal attributes of the world around us. Hence, this book was born.

# TABLE OF CONTENTS

# INTRODUCTION

Tired of always looking for certain spells or rituals and never really finding what you need? Then it's time that you started writing your own personal spells, and this guide can help you do that.

The biggest obstacle of creating a spell is knowing what materials are used for what purpose, so I've collected a huge number of magickal correspondences to guide you in putting together any type of spell you could want.

This book isn't going to hold your hand and tell you how much of what item needs to be used to have a certain outcome. Consider this a guide to a wide range of magickal ingredients so that you can choose which things go in your spells. How you decide to mix them into a ritual is up to you. I do have a quick chapter on putting it all together, but the main point here is to give you a really handy bunch of correspondences without all the extra fluff that so many print books give you.

I have included basically anything and everything you would want to incorporate into a ritual, yet only the things you are likely to be able to get. What's the point of knowing the magickal properties of some rare orchid that you'll never see in your lifetime?

This is a practical and to-the-point guide to direct you in building your own successful spells.

The first section is broken down by *type* of item, such as herbs, stones, colors, planets and more. This is where you can take some ingredient that you have and see what it can offer you.

Secondly is a section based on *purpose*. This is probably where you'll do your first research into a new spell, by looking for your intention. I have all the big purposes listed but some of the lesser ones aren't included. But you can still read through the first section to find out more. For example, the herb basil is excellent at helping to mend conflicts between people and the entry for basil says so. But I don't have a specific purpose section listed for "healing conflicts".

Enough chatter. This guide should be easy enough to navigate without any further explanations, so keep reading and get ready to start building your own unique spells.

# Section 1
## Spell Materials, Ingredients and Influences

This is the section organized by the type of item or influence you want to have in your spell. All the common (and not so common) supplies are listed here and you can see what magick they all hold.

# 1 HERBS

This is the section you'll use for any herb-based materials, so that includes actual herbs as well as oils, incense and tinctures. The energy in the plant will be the same regardless of its form. Various resins and gums have also been included here since they don't really fit anywhere else.

When using actual herbs, fresh is usually better but it really depends on the type of spell you're doing. Sometimes dried or powdered can do the job better (not to mention that dried herbs are a lot easier to find and store).

Remember that this is a list of magickal correspondences, and should not be considered a medical herbal in anyway. Many of these herbs are toxic and are not supposed to be taken internally, and that goes for the ones that may be good for healing magick. That doesn't not mean they are *medically* healthy for you.

## *Plants and Flowers*

Acacia.................................protection, psychic talents, prosperity, friendship

Adam & Eve Root..........love, passion

Adders' Tongue...............healing, divination, stops gossip

Agrimony...........................protection, banishing, removing negative energy, sleep, breaking hexes

Allspice..............................prosperity, courage, power, energy

Aloe..................................healing, luck, peace, home protection

Amaranth..........................mending heartbreak, protection

Angelica............................protection, health, divination, banishing spirits

Anise.................................purification, protection, psychic talents

Asafoetida.........................banishing, protection (Extremely foul smelling. Use with caution!)

Balm of Gilead.................protection, healing, love

Barley................................honor the harvest, protection

Basil..................................heal conflicts, sympathy, happiness, prosperity, banish spirits

Bay...................................protection, psychic talents, purification, good luck

Bedstraw...........................love

Belladonna........................astral travel, ingredient in flying ointments

Benzoin (resin)................prosperity, astral travel, purification, relieving stress, divination

Bergamot..........................prosperity, success

Betony..............................peaceful sleep, happiness, purification, healing

Bittersweet.......................protection, healing

Black Cohosh...................strength, fertility, love

Blessed Thistle................protection, cleansing, break hexes

Bloodroot.........................love, purification

Bluebells...........................good luck, friendship, peace of mind

Borage..............................psychic talents, prosperity, courage, strength

Broom..............................wedding blessings, weather magick, used to make besoms, divination

Buckthorn........................hex breaking, banish negative energy, legal matters

Burdock............................cleansing, protection

Calamus............................good luck, prosperity, success

Calendula.........................legal matters, protection, psychic talents

Camphor............................health, purity, divination, psychic talents

Caraway..............................passion, creativity, protection

Cardamom.........................passion, love, fertility

Carnation...........................female energy, healing, strength, creativity

Catnip................................cat magick, love, beauty, happiness

Cayenne.............................purification, banish negative energy

Chamomile........................love, friendship, meditation, peace, sleep

Chicory..............................good luck, overcoming obstacles, influence others

Chervl...............................spiritual growth, divination, spirit communication

Chrysanthemum..............protection

Cinnamon.........................energy, passion, creativity, spiritual growth, psychic talents, prosperity

Cinquefoil.........................prosperity, sleep, dreams, protection, love

Cloves...............................banishing, love, passion, protection

Clover...............................protection, success, love, luck

Coltsfoot............................love, psychic talents, peace

Comfrey............................safe travel, prosperity, legal matters

Copal (resin).....................purification, cleansing

Coriander..........................healing, love, protection, peace

Cowslip............................healing, uncovering hidden mysteries, youth, home blessings

Cumin..............................protection, banishing spirits

Curry................................protection, banishing spirits, hex breaking

Cypress.............................healing, protection, peace, overcoming a loss

Daffodil............................fertility, luck, love

Damiana...........................love, passion, romance

Dandelion........................divination, good luck, psychic talents

Devil's Shoestring............luck, gambling, prosperity, employment

Dill...................................prosperity, luck, protection, passion

Dragon's Blood (resin)...love, banishing spirits, strength

Elder................................banishing spirits, healing, sleep, home blessings

Elecampane......................love, psychic talents, banishing negative energy

Eucalyptus........................healing, protection

Evening Primrose.............fairy magick, love, beauty

Eyebright..........................psychic talents, creativity, divination

Fennel...............................protection, healing, strength, purification

Fern...................................bringing rain, prosperity, healing, good luck, mental focus

Feverfew...........................protection, healing, safe travel

Flax....................................prosperity, psychic talents, beauty

Foxglove...........................protection, spirit communication

Frankincense (resin)........purification, spiritual growth, banishing spirits

Galangal............................psychic talents, luck, prosperity, break hexes, legal matters

Gardenia............................healing, love, peace, spiritual growth

Garlic................................protection, passion, healing, banishing spirits, cleansing

Geranium..........................fertility, healing, love, positive thinking

Ginger...............................success, courage, strength, prosperity, passion

Ginseng.............................luck, beauty, passion, success

Goldenseal........................healing, prosperity, success

Gum Arabic (resin).........see acacia

Gum Mastic (resin).........passion, psychic talents

Hawthorn..........................fertility, purity, happiness, fairy magick, employment

Heather..............................new beginnings, rain magick, peace, protection

Heliotrope.........................banishing spirits, psychic talents, prosperity, happiness, solar energy

Hemlock............................purification, cooling emotions

Henbane............................love, purification

Hibiscus.............................passion, love, dreams

High John..........................success, prosperity, luck, gambling, protection

Holly..................................protection, luck, lightening protection, dreams

Honeysuckle......................love, healing, creativity, psychic talents

Hops..................................dreams, peace

Horehound......................banishing spirits, clear thinking,
protection

Hyacinth...........................love, happiness, peace, luck

Hyssop.............................purification, removing negative energy

Iris....................................purification, knowledge, wisdom

Irish Moss........................protection, luck, prosperity, gambling

Ivy....................................love, fertility, banish negative energy,
weddings

Jasmine............................love, passion, dreams

Job's Tears.......................employment, good luck, prosperity

Juniper.............................cleansing, purification, love, banishing
spirits, healing

Knotweed.........................binding magick, hexes

Larkspur...........................health, protection

Lavender...........................love, sleep, dreams, meditation,
purity, health, peace

Lemon Balm.....................love, success, healing, psychic talents

Lemongrass......................psychic talents, passion

Lemon Verbena.................purification, love

Licorice.............................passion, fidelity, love

Lilac....................................protection, sleep, divination, beauty,
wisdom

Lily......................................protection, weddings, fidelity, fertility,
happiness

Lotus...................................overcoming obstacles, protection,
peace

Lovage...............................dreams, psychic talents, beauty

Lucky Hand.....................success, luck, gambling, travel

Mace...................................psychic talents, creativity, mental
focus

Magnolia...........................fidelity

Mandrake..........................protection, good health, love, fertility,
banishing spirits

Marigold........................... legal issues, divination, dreams,
psychic talents

Marjoram..........................protection, happiness, luck,
prosperity, dreams

Meadowsweet..................love, peace, calm homes, friendship

Mimosa.............................protection, dreams, purification, love

Mint.................................prosperity, creativity, healing, luck, travel, banishing spirits

Mistletoe..........................fertility, banishing spirits, protection, healing, creativity

Morning Glory.................binding, banishing

Mugwort...........................protection, divination, psychic talents, healing, success

Mullein.............................courage, protection, banishing spirits, dreams

Myrrh (resin)....................healing, spiritual growth, purification

Myrtle...............................love, fertility, peace, youth

Narcissus...........................peace

Nettle...............................protection, passion, banishing spirits, stops gossip

Nutmeg............................prosperity, protection, hex breaking

Oakmoss...........................luck, prosperity, strength

Orchid..............................love, mental focus

Orris Root........................love, passion, protection, influencing others

Parsley..............................love, purification, peace, fertility

Patchouli............................passion, prosperity, fertility

Pennyroyal.........................strength, protection, peace, home
blessings

Pepper (black)...................banishing spirits, protection,
purification

Pine....................................prosperity, healing, fertility, banishing
spirits, grounding

Plantain.............................healing, strength, protection, home
blessings

Plumeria.............................love, influencing others, friendship

Poke Root..........................finding lost items, hex breaking,
strength

Poppy.................................fertility, sleep, prosperity, love

Purslane.............................sleep, protection, luck

Rice....................................fertility, prosperity

Rose...................................love, friendship, healing, psychic
talents

Rose Geranium.................stops gossip, banishing negative
energy

Rosemary...........................purification, banishing spirits,
cleansing, healing, passion, mental focus

Rowan..............................psychic talents, creativity, prosperity, banish spirits

Rue..............................banishing, protection, healing, psychic talents

Saffron..............................love, happiness, healing, passion, luck

Sage..............................wisdom, protection, luck, overcoming loss, mental focus

Sandalwood..............................spiritual growth, banishing spirits, healing, purification

Sassafras..............................healing, prosperity, overcoming addictions

Savory..............................creativity, psychic talents, passion

Scullcap..............................fidelity, home blessings, peace

Snakeroot..............................passion, love, prosperity

Solomon's Seal..............................protection, banishing spirits, bindings

Star Anise..............................protection, banishing spirits, psychic talents, luck

St. John's Wort..............................healing, protection, love, divination

Sweetgrass..............................divination, psychic talents, peace

Tansy..............................healing, long life, banishing spirits

Tarragon............................emotional healing, empathy

Thyme...............................sleep, strength, protection, love,
purification

Tobacco............................healing, purification, strength

Tonka Beans.....................good luck, love, prosperity

Tuberose...........................passion, peace, romance

Turmeric...........................purification

Valerian.............................love, sleep, protection, dreams,
reconciliation

Vanilla...............................passion, courage, love, psychic talents

Vervain..............................prosperity, sleep, healing, creativity,
love, long life

Vetivert..............................breaking hexes, protection, good luck,
prosperity

Violet................................protection, good luck, peace, healing,
dreams

White Sage........................purification, removes negative energy

Witch Hazel......................protection, purity, overcoming loss

Wood Aloe........................protection, purification, prosperity

Woodruff..........................success, prosperity

Wolfsbane...........................cleansing, purification, protect from werewolves

Wormwood......................divination, banishing spirits, psychic talents, calm, safe travel

Yarrow..............................love, banishing, psychic talents, healing, weddings

Yerba Mate.......................love, passion, fidelity

Ylang-Ylang......................passion, love, fairy magick, peace

## *Trees*

I'm adding a little sub-section on trees even though they are not usually used in the same way as most herbs. Leaves would work if you have them but most people use pieces of wood to harness the energy of a tree.

Alder..................................divination, learning, choices

Ash....................................protection, prosperity, the sea

Aspen................................communication, psychic talents

Birch..................................banishing spirits, protection, purification

Beech.................................good luck, divination, creativity

Cedar............................home blessings, good luck, prosperity, purification

Elm....................................love, stop gossip

Hazel...............................divination, psychic talents, dreams, lightening protection, good luck

Hickory...............................legal issues, communication, passion

Maple................................healing, love

Oak..................................... protection, fertility, luck, prosperity

Walnut..............................spiritual growth, good luck

Willow...............................divination, love, healing, happiness

## *Fruits and Nuts*

While technically not herbs, and not often used in spellcraft, I thought I would include a little section on fruits and nuts.

 Many do have magickal histories to them and can make great Deity offerings even if you're not using fruit in any specific spells.

Acorn................................luck, wisdom, protection

Almond.............................prosperity, wisdom, healing, overcoming addictions

Apple...............................love, healing, plant magick, fertility

Avocado...........................passion, love, beauty

Banana.............................fertility, prosperity

Blueberry.........................protection

Brazil nuts.......................love, relationships

Cashew.............................prosperity

Cherry.............................happiness, divination, love

Chestnut...........................love

Fig....................................fertility, love, divination

Grape...............................fertility, creativity, psychic talents,
prosperity

Lemon.............................friendship, love, purification

Lime.................................healing, protection, peace

Olive................................fidelity, marriage, fertility

Orange.............................happiness, purification, divination

Pecan...............................employment, prosperity

Plum................................healing, peace

Pomegranate...................divination, luck, prosperity

Pumpkin............................lunar energy, divination, psychic talents

Strawberry.........................luck, childbirth, success

Walnut...............................spiritual growth, luck

# 2 STONES & CRYSTALS

Crystals of many kinds are frequently used in spells, particularly those where you need to carry a charm of some sort with you.

Stones can come in many forms, usually either raw crystals or as smooth tumbled pieces. You should buy your crystals from a reputable dealer to make sure you are in fact buying the mineral you think you are.

You may notice that many of these stones have a diverse range of uses. Don't be surprised if you have to experiment a little to find what works best for you. Correspondences for crystals tend to be more personal, and stones will react differently with different people.

Amazonite........................strength, peace, calming, healing, creativity

Amber...............................solar energy, protection, spirituality, purification

Amethyst..........................dreams, meditation, divination, imagination, creativity, astral travel, mental focus

Aquamarine......................divination, relaxation, freeing blocked energy, eloquence

Aventurine.......................prosperity, fertility, abundance, emotional healing, awareness, independence

Azurite..............................psychic talents, divination, dreams, wisdom, intuition

Beryl.................................divination, wisdom, intelligence

Bloodstone.......................strength, confidence, luck, energy, prosperity, long life, legal matters

Blue Lace Agate...............female energy, relaxation, peace

Botswana Agate...............emotional healing

Calcite..............................cleansing, purifying

Carnelian..........................psychic talents, sexuality, eases anger, ambition, peace

Celestite...........................astral travel, dreams, meditation

Chalcedony.......................protection, eases fears, safe travel, dreams

Chrysocolla.......................controlling emotions, peace, wisdom, awareness, balance

Citrine..............................energy, hope, beginnings, sleep, creativity, happiness

Coral.................................safe travel, protection, love, dreams

Diamond...........................purity, abundance, fidelity

Emerald.............................love, peace, communication, psychic talents, patience

Fluorite.............................creativity, meditation, mental focus, learning, intelligence

Garnet.............................passion, fertility, prosperity, strength, friendship, peace, dreams

Hematite..........................grounding, healing, balance, protection, divination

Jade.................................prosperity, balance, long life, luck, healing, safe travel

Jet...................................protection, Goddess spirituality, divination, healing

Kunzite............................communication, banishing, mental focus

Kyanite............................calming, peace, inspiration, communication

Labradorite......................imagination, freedom, spirit communication, balance

Lapis Lazuli.....................psychic talents, enlightenment, love, peace, spirituality

Lodestone.........................drawing energy to you, prosperity, luck

Malachite..........................prosperity, business, finances, luck, fidelity, transformation

Moldavite...........................spiritual communication, psychic talents, awareness

Moonstone.......................Lunar energy, psychic talents, mental focus, peace, nurturing

Moss Agate.......................plants, friendship, cleansing, long life

Obsidian............................protection, strength, absorbs energy, grounding

Onyx.................................protection, endurance, learning, banishing negativity

Pearl..................................feminine energy, love, marriage, strength, fertility

Peridot..............................psychic talents, dreams, inspiration, protection, confidence

Pyrite.................................prosperity, finances, communication, luck, energy

Quartz...............................any sort of magickal working

Red Jasper.........................passion, dreams, health, energy

Rhodonite.........................mental focus, clarity, peace, confidence

Rose Quartz.....................love, healing, friendship, peace, happiness, fidelity

Ruby.................................prosperity, protection, confidence, love, honesty

Salt....................................purification, cleansing, grounding

Sapphire............................peace, calming, metal focus, spirituality

Selenite..............................decisions, balance, mental focus, luck

Smoky Quartz..................energy, strength, grounding

Sodalite.............................courage, intellect, safe travel, emotional healing, communication

Sugalite.............................psychic talents, healing, spirituality, enlightenment

Tiger Eye...........................balance, meditation, new business ventures, grounding, luck

Topaz................................dreams, banishing negativity, safe travel, calming, peace

Tourmaline.......................banishing negativity

Turquoise..........................psychic protection, divination, fidelity, relationships

Unakite.............................awareness, personal growth, balancing emotions

# 3 COLORS

Colors all have their own energy, and they offer you an easy way to tailor your spells to a purpose just by controlling what color items you are using.

These are the associations with the main colors of the spectrum. I've left out various shades and blends, and stuck with these base colors. One exception is pink. Though it's just a lighter version of red, it has long had its own magickal correspondences that should be mentioned.

## *Red*

- Love
- Passion
- Strength
- Joy
- Energy
- Desires
- Sexuality
- Courage
- Conflicts

## *Orange*

- Abundance
- Motivation
- Justice
- Luck

- Prosperity
- Accomplishments
- Opportunities
- Legal issues

## *Yellow*

- Communication
- Intelligence
- Concentration
- Focus
- Confidence
- Positive thinking
- Beauty
- Learning
- Wisdom
- Humility

## *Green*

- Prosperity
- Finances
- Employment
- Career
- Ambition
- Success
- Fertility
- Business
- Nature
- Social activities
- Fairies
- Herbal magick

## Blue

- Spirituality
- Wisdom
- Friendship
- Inspiration
- Creativity
- Acceptance
- Self-improvement
- Religion
- Peace
- Philosophy
- Healing

## Purple

- Spirituality
- Psychic talents
- Divination
- Messages
- Healing
- Development
- Intelligence
- Emotional healing
- Peace
- Studying
- Memory

## Black

- Grounding
- Banishing
- Death

- Protection
- Binding
- Endings
- Divination
- Rebirth
- Legal issues
- Difficulties
- Obstacles

## *White*

- Purity
- Peace
- Safety
- Enlightenment
- Protection
- Moon energy
- Spirituality
- Beginnings
- Multi-purpose in any spell

## *Brown*

- Earth energy
- Grounding
- Endurance
- Animals
- Nature
- Abundance
- Friendship
- Harvests
- Security
- Lost items

# *Pink*

- Friendship
- Happiness
- Peace
- Harmony
- Purity
- Affection
- Contentment
- Fidelity
- New romance

# *Gold*

- God/male energy
- Good luck
- Success
- Sun energy
- Home blessings
- Ambition
- Wealth
- Safety

# *Silver*

- Goddess/female energy
- Reflection
- Moon energy
- Psychic talents
- Meditation
- Relaxation
- Protection

# 4 ELEMENTS

The 4 traditional elements that make up our physical world can be seen as the basis for most correspondences. Many items are related through their elemental connections, and you'll find that this is the point where you start to see how natural features related to one another.

Because of the foundational nature of the elements, I'm giving a complete picture of each one with all the different correspondences tied together here.

Though you don't often need to take your Zodiac sign into account for spellwork, if you are working on any sort of personal development or changes, this can be a good way to tune your spell towards your personal energies.

## *Fire*

**Colors**: red, orange

**Attributes**: strength, passion, anger, energy, creativity, destruction, ambition, purification, confidence

**Herbs:** basil, hibiscus, woodruff, cedar, nutmeg, rosemary, cinnamon, nettle, pepper, clove, dill, fennel, tobacco

**Stones**: bloodstone, red jasper, garnet, carnelian, opals, amber, tiger eye, obsidian

**Altar representations**: candles, athame (in some traditions), lamps

**Astrological sign**: Aries, Leo Sagittarius

**Direction**: south

**Mythical beings**: salamanders, dragons


## *Air*

**Colors**: white, silver, yellow

**Attributes**: travel, intellect, wisdom, mental abilities, communication, ideas, creativity, dreams, learning, psychic talents

**Herbs**: mint, pine, yarrow, lemongrass, sage, pansy, lavender, vervain, mistletoe, acacia, violet, marjoram, frankincense, myrrth

**Stones:** amethyst, clear quartz, labradorite, fluorite, topaz

**Altar representations**: wand, feathers, bells, incense, flags

**Astrological sign**: Aquarius, Gemini, Libra

**Direction**: east

**Mythical beings**: sylphs, fairies

## *Water*

**Colors**: blue, purple

**Attributes**: love, healing, friendship, emotions, fertility, mystery, sleep, compassion, empathy, sorrow

**Herbs**: valerian, rose, lotus, chamomile, orris, sandalwood, lilac, jasmine, gardenia, water lilies, licorice, peach, vanilla

**Stones**: jade, moonstone, aquamarine, lapis lazuli, citrine

**Altar representations**: dish of water, chalice, cauldron, mirrors, coral

**Astrological sign**: Pisces, Cancer, Scorpio

**Direction**: west

**Mythical beings**: nymphs, undines, mermaids


## *Earth*

**Colors**: brown, green

**Attributes**: nature, animals, grounding, finances, abundance, prosperity, growth, responsibility, protection

**Herbs**: mugwort, cypress, honeysuckle, patchouli, grains, oakmoss, vetivert, comfrey

**Stones**: aventurine, onyx, jet, peridot, moss agate, emerald, malachite, hematite

**Altar representations**: bowl of earth, salt, pentacle, acorns, live plant

**Astrological sign**: Taurus, Virgo, Capricorn

**Direction**: north

**Mythical beings**: gnomes, dwarfs

# 5 DAYS OF THE WEEK

Though the entire concept of "days of the week" is a man-made one, there have long been certain associations with each day that can be used in magick. When planning out your spells, you can add to their energy if you perform them on the right days.

First, here are the roots for each of the names we use today. They are named after planets and Norse Gods (not sure *why* there is such a mix).

Monday – the Moon
Tuesday - Tyr
Wednesday - Woden
Thursday - Thor
Friday - Frigga
Saturday - Saturn
Sunday – the Sun

And here are the main correspondences for the days, along with the main planet that rules each day:

## *Monday (the Moon)*

- Spirituality
- Astral work
- Dreams
- Psychic talents
- Lunar energy

- Family
- Emotions
- Children
- Pets
- Fertility
- Female Energy
- Purification
- Wisdom

## *Tuesday (Mars)*

- Strength
- Anger
- Independence
- Motivation
- Conquest
- Action
- Education
- Force
- Handling conflict

## *Wednesday (Mercury)*

- Creativity
- Divination
- Employment
- Knowledge
- Travel
- Communication
- Wisdom
- Learning
- Addictions
- Business
- Negotiations

# Thursday (Jupiter)

- Prosperity
- Wealth
- Growth
- Luck
- Male energy
- Debts
- Finances
- Development
- Legal issues

# Friday (Venus)

- Love
- Peace
- Family
- Marriage
- Beauty
- Growth
- Art
- Social status
- Passion
- Music
- Sexuality

# Saturday (Saturn)

- Banishing
- Protection
- Bindings

- Lost objects
- Discipline
- Habits
- Freedom
- Obstacles
- Endings
- Spirit communication
- Meditation

## Sunday (the Sun)

- Health
- Abundance
- Leadership
- Strength
- Ambition
- Individuality
- Authority
- Hope
- Happiness
- Creativity

# 6 DIRECTIONS

You might not use these correspondences as often as the others, but they can be just as fundamental as the elements themselves. Directions can be used in any spell where you can choose which way you wish to face, or which way you have your altar facing. These also come into play when you call the quarters to form a sacred circle.

Note that these attributes are not universal. Though South is almost always associated with fire attributes, the other directions are more flexible. What I'm giving here is a Celtic version though your own tradition may hold the directions to different traits.

## *North*

**Colors**: brown, black

**Attributes:** grounding, animals, nature, fertility, darkness, wisdom, discovery, prosperity, abundance

**Herbs:** patchouli, vetivert, mugwort, oakmoss

**Stones:** onyx, malachite, peridot, jet, hematite

**Element:** Earth

## South

**Colors**: red, orange

**Attributes**: passion, sexuality, energy, courage, strength, love, success, fidelity, cleansing

**Herbs**: nettle, pepper, basil, fennel, woodruff, tobacco

**Stones**: garnet, amber, tiger eye, bloodstone

**Element**: Fire


## East

**Colors**: yellow, pink, white

**Attributes**: creativity, inspiration, wisdom, youth, intelligence, learning, beginnings, awareness

**Herbs**: mint, sage, lavender, violet, yarrow

**Stones**: quartz, amethyst, fluorite, topaz

**Element: Air**


## West

**Colors**: blue, purple

**Attributes**: dreams, mystery, psychic talents, emotions, sleep, healing, friendship

**Herbs**: lotus, chamomile, orris, jasmine, lilac, gardenia

**Stones**: moonstone, aquamarine, jade, citrine

**Element**: Water

# 7 PLANETS

Harnessing the energy of the planets comes into play mostly with astrological studies, and you can arrange your spellwork based the positions of bodies in the heavens. It also creates another level of connection between attributes.

I'm including the sun and moon even though they are not actually planets. I'm also well aware that Pluto is no longer technically a planet, but it has always been considered to have some distant influence, and will continue to do so regardless of the label we give it.

## *Mercury*

**Attributes**: communication, creativity, divination, thankfulness, mental focus, changes

**Element**: Air

**Herbs**: lavender, lemongrass, peppermint

**Stones**: fluorite, agate, aventurine

**Day**: Wednesday

## *Venus*

**Attributes**: love, romance, beauty, art of all kinds, harmony, sensuality, fertility, partnerships

**Element**: Water

**Herbs**: rose, yarrow, damiana

**Stones**: jade, rose quartz, turquoise

**Day**: Friday


## *Mars*

**Attributes**: courage, passion, male energy, protection, victory, ambitions, success, conflict

**Element**: Fire

**Herbs**: dragon's blood resin, pine, wormwood

**Stones**: bloodstone, red jasper, garnet

**Day**: Tuesday


## *Jupiter*

**Attributes**: legal matters, business, growth, prosperity, power, agreements, organizations

**Elements**: Air and Fire

**Herbs**: cedar, sage, nutmeg

**Stones**: sodalite, lapis lazuli, sapphire

**Day**: Thursday


## *Saturn*

**Attributes**: knowledge, endings, protection, banishings, depression, lost things

**Elements**: Earth and Water

**Herbs**: patchouli, mandrake, comfrey

**Stones**: onyx, lodestone, hematite

**Day**: Saturday


## *Sun*

**Attributes**: success, power, growth, leadership, pride, ambition, health, family, confidence

**Element**: Fire

**Herbs**: cinnamon, orange, frankincense, cloves

**Stones**: carnelian, tiger eye, amber

**Day**: Sunday

## *Moon*

**Attributes**: psychic talents, sleep, dreams, safe travel, understanding, inspiration, fertility

**Element**: Water

**Herbs**: lotus, vervain, chamomile, jasmine

**Stones**: moonstone, aquamarine, pearl, amethyst

**Day**: Monday

The next three are not as often considered in magickal workings, but I figured they should be included anyway. It's only fair.

## *Neptune*

**Attributes**: Dreams, creativity, friendship, ideas, confusion, empathy, carelessness

**Element**: Water

**Herbs**: Lily, carnation, parsley, ferns, pine

**Stones**: amethyst, coral, jade

**Day**: none

## Uranus

**Attributes**: Independence, freedom, rebellion, change

**Element:** Air

**Herbs**: rosemary, woodruff, mistletoe

**Stones**: aventurine, diamond, amethyst

**Day**: none


## Pluto

**Attributes**: mystery, the unknown, self awareness, spirituality, rebirth

**Element**: Water

**Herbs**: nettle, wormwood, mandrake, hemlock

**Stones**: jet, bloodstone, onyx

**Day**: none

# 8 ANIMALS

Like the herbs chapter, this one could conceivably go on forever. Though all animals have their own power and energy, certain ones are more commonly used in any sort of magickal or spiritual working. So I've chosen the most likely ones that you will want to know about.

Many animals are sacred to certain Deities, even though their qualities aren't always the same.

You will also find that some animals are important in more than one belief system, or culture, and that can lead to varying attributes. In many cases, animals simply represent strength, wisdom and the natural world. It's not always complicated.

You can look at these correspondences in two ways. They can be used to interpret signs when you see animals unexpectedly in the wild, but they can also tell you more about a totem animal or familiar that you may want to work with.

Alligator................. patience, energy, frugality, birth and death

Antelope................caution, instincts, escapes

Badger.................... tenacity, endurance, strength, protector

Bat...........................the underworld, messages, clarity

Bear.........................perseverance, wisdom, strength, stamina, courage (Odin)

Bee...........................communication, hard work (Venus)

Beetle......................past lives, reincarnation, rebirth, awareness

Blackbird...............the spirit world

Bluebird.................happiness, contentment, satisfaction

Bull.........................virility, strength, expansion, movement

Butterfly.................transformation, inner beauty, joy, changes, the arts

Cat...........................grace, hidden knowledge, independence, sensuality, the spirit world (Bast)

Cheetah..................speed, stealth, endurance

Chickadee..............truth, knowledge

Cougar...................power, mystery, independence, grace

Cow.........................abundance, love, family, stubbornness (Hathor)

Coyote....................cunning, dreams, instincts, awareness, tricks

Crane......................magickal secrets, hidden mysteries, healing, travel

Cricket...................good luck, travel, messages

Crow......................wisdom, darkness, conflict, messages, the dead (Morrigan, Hecate)

Deer........................family, peace, trust, pregnancy, innocence (Artemis, Aphrodite)

Dog........................protection, loyalty, friendship, devotion, compassion, hunting

Dolphin..................messages, water energy, harmony (Apollo)

Donkey..................decision making, stubbornness, opinions

Dove......................love, peace, relationships

Dragonfly..............reflections, energy of light, beauty, dreams

Duck......................family, motherhood, protection

Eagle......................wisdom, patience, long life, knowledge, clarity

Elephant................strength, wisdom, age, grounding

Fox........................trickery, quick-thinking, family, staying at a distance, stealth

Frog......................fertility, home, illusion, emotions

Goat......................independence, confidence

Grasshopper..........faith, determination, psychic talents

Hare......................fertility, lunar energy, re-birth, speed (Eostre, Aphrodite)

Hawk......................signals and signs, quick action

Heron......................see Crane

Horse......................fertility, energy, endurance, faith, freedom (Epona)

Hummingbird.......joy, peace, love

Jaguar......................courage, psychic talents, the spirit world

Kangaroo...............family, protection, safety

Leopard.................silence, patience

Lion.......................family, relaxation, indulgence

Lizards...................prosperity, the unconscious, small details

Magpie...................omens, signs, divination, portents

Monkey.................play, happiness, intelligence

Mouse...................overcoming obstacles, secrets, hiding (Apollo)

Nightingale...........love, freedom (Adonis)

Opossum............... practicality, recovery

Orca......................healing, protection, divination

Otter......................playfulness, loving life, communication with other worlds

Owl........................wisdom, vision, truth, awareness, silence (Athena)

Panther...................see Jaguar

Peacock.................warnings, psychic talents (Hera)

Pig...........................rebirth

Quail......................peace, serenity

Rabbit.....................see Hare

Raccoon.................cleverness, creativity, inquisitiveness, new opportunities

Raven......................see Crow

Robin......................new life, growth (Thor)

Shark......................knowledge, silence, ruthlessness, immediate action

Sheep.....................meekness, fertility, family, new life

Skunk.....................unseen strength, inner power

Snake.....................secrets, transformations, healing (Hermes, Ra)

Sparrow.................new ideas, awakening, discovery

Spider.....................fate, destiny, future, wisdom

Squirrel...................being prepared, resource,s discoveries

Starling...................intelligence, change, social groups

Stork.......................birth, family, new beginnings

Swan.......................dreams, transitions, changes, spirituality,
purity

Tiger.......................energy, power, spirituality

Turtle......................the Earth itself, creative change,
motherhood, long life

Vulture...................purification, rebirth

Whale.....................long life, family

Wolf........................loyalty, knowledge, solitary, lunar energy

Woodpecker..........portents, messages

Wren.......................divination, cleansing


## Mythical Beasts

Needless to say, you won't be coming across these out in the
wild but you may catch glimpses of them during astral
travelling, meditation or dreams. Knowing their symbolism can
still be helpful.

Centaur..................creativity, the arts, psychic talents

Dragon..................transformations, spirituality, long life, abundance, success

Griffin...................clarity, understanding, awareness

Minotaur...............protection, power, fertility

Pegasus.................psychic talents, love, creativity

Phoenix.................rebirth, new beginnings, changes, flexibility

Unicorn.................success, abundance, purity, cleansing

# 9 ZODIAC SIGNS

Anyone who does a lot of work with astrology will want to know what materials and magickal supplies are tied to their personal Zodiac signs. When doing any spells that impact you personally, it can be a nice approach to attune your materials to your astrological sign as well as the spell's overall purpose.

## *Aries*

**Birthdates**: March 21$^{st}$ to April 9$^{th}$

**Attributes**: Ambitious, organized, logical, generous, childish, leadership

**Herbs**: Thistle, holly, chestnut, wormwood, dragon's blood, damiana

**Stones**: Ruby, garnet, bloodstone, diamond

**Element**: Fire

**Day**: Tuesday

**Colors**: Red, pink, white

**Planet**: Mars

## *Taurus*

**Birthdates**: April 20<sup>th</sup> to May 20<sup>th</sup>

**Attributes**: Patient, logical, tidy, grounded, stable, quiet

**Herbs**: Violet, almond, rose, thyme, jasmine, honeysuckle

**Stones**: Emerald, turquoise, jade

**Element**: Earth

**Day**: Friday

**Colors**: Blue, green

**Planet**: Earth


## *Gemini*

**Birthdates**: May 21<sup>st</sup> to June 20th

**Attributes**: Creative, moody, positive, changeable, charismatic

**Herbs**: Dill, fern, licorice, sage, sandalwood, cinquefoil

**Stones**: Agate, topaz, carnelian

**Element**: Air

**Day**: Wednesday

**Colors**: White, yellow, silver

**Planet**: Mercury

## Cancer

**Birthdates**: June 21st to July 22nd

**Attributes**: Sensitive, emotional, practical, organized, routine

**Herbs**: Poppy, willow, lemon balm, mugwort, orris

**Stones**: Emerald, moonstone, pearl

**Element**: Water

**Day**: Monday

**Colors**: Silver, pale blue

**Planet**: Moon


## Leo

**Birthdates**: July 23rd to August 22nd

**Attributes**: Bold, spendthrift, ambitious, courageous, vain

**Herbs**: Sunflower, hops, copal resin, angelica, rue

**Stones**: Ruby, amber, citrine, topaz

**Element**: Fire

**Day**: Sunday

**Colors**: Yellow, red, orange

**Planet**: Sun

## Virgo

**Birthdates**: August 23rd to September 22nd

**Attributes**: Logical, quiet, intellectual, detailed, obsessive

**Herbs**: Rosemary, valerian, meadowsweet, dill, chamomile

**Stones**: Carnelian, jasper, sapphire

**Element**: Earth

**Day**: Wednesday

**Colors**: Peach, yellow, light blue

**Planet**: Mercury


## Libra

**Birthdates**: September 23rd to October 22nd

**Attributes**: Balanced, committed, lazy, luxurious, indecisive

**Herbs**: Violet, hyacinth, pansy, orris, mint, burdock

**Stones**: Opal, peridot, lapis, tourmaline

**Element**: Air

**Day**: Friday

**Colors**: Deep blue, green

**Planet**: Venus

# Scorpio

**Birthdates**: October 23rd to November 21st

**Attributes**: Perfectionist, flexible, jealous, clever, intense

**Herbs**: Basil, holly, tobacco, vanilla, ginseng

**Stones**: Topaz, jet, ruby, opal, obsidian

**Element**: Water

**Day**: Tuesday

**Colors**: Red, black, brown

**Planet**: Mars, Pluto


# Sagittarius

**Birthdates**: November 22nd to December 21st

**Attributes**: Adventurous, friendly, honest, unpredictable, chatty

**Herbs**: Sage, carnation, cedar, lilac, sandalwood, pine

**Stones**: Amethyst, topaz, turquoise, lapiz lazuli

**Element**: Fire

**Day**: Thursday

**Colors**: Purple, indigo, lavender

**Planet**: Jupiter

# Capricorn

**Birthdates**: December 22nd to January 19th

**Attributes**: Intelligent, organized, stubborn, loner, impulsive

**Herbs**: rue, cypress, garlic, myrrh, lobelia

**Stones**: Onyx, jet, opal, garnet

**Element**: Earth

**Day**: Saturday

**Colors**: Black, brown, purple

**Planet**: Saturn


# Aquarius

**Birthdates**: January 20th to February 18th

**Attributes**: Controlling, unusual, social, open-minded, leadership

**Herbs**: foxglove, pine, nutmeg, curry, allspice

**Stones**: amber, malachite, aquamarine, turquoise

**Element**: Air

**Day**: Saturday

**Colors**: All colors

**Planet**: Saturn and Uranus

## *Pisces*

**Birthdates**: February 19th to March 20th

**Attributes**: Sensitive, creative, impulsive, quick-thinking, artistic

**Herbs**: carnation, willow, mugwort, lovage, lavender, hops

**Stones:** sapphire, amethyst, moonstone

**Element**: Water

**Day**: Thursday

**Colors**: green, white, purple

**Planet**: Jupiter and Neptune

# 10 GODS & GODDESSES

Not everyone works with the Gods (or Goddesses) when they cast spells, but they can be a powerful addition to any ritual. Knowing what they represent can help you know who to call on when you have a request.

Just remember that drawing a name out of the blue and asking for assistance is a little impolite. And also, these figures are more than just cardboard cut-outs that "rule" over certain things. I'm taking that approach when presenting them in this book because that's the purpose here, but these are full-fledged beings that are more than just a list of attributes. There are also relationships between them that I'm not mentioning here to keep things simple.

Many Deities had functions in the world, like ruling the afterlife or controlling the crops, and aren't really seen as ruling over certain *attributes*. That doesn't necessarily mean they can't help you with certain things, just that you need to understand their roles. You aren't going to find a simple list here like the other chapters is what I'm getting at.

I've broken this section up by cultural pantheon, but the Gods and Goddesses are mixed together. The m or f at the end indicates if they are male or female. You wouldn't want to call a Goddess "he", would you?

The first 4 pantheons are the most commonly involved in modern-day Pagan worship and spellwork. The deities for Santeria and Vodou are well-known enough in the Pagan world but are typically not invoked unless you are strictly following those particular paths. So for the purpose of this book, I'm just going to stick to the main 4.

## *Egyptian*

Amun / Aten..................creation, the sun (m)

Anubis.............................the underworld, alchemy, spirits of the dead, medicine, travel, justice (m)

Bast....................................cats, childbirth, sexuality, passion, lunar energy, joy, humour, home protection (f)

Bes....................................protection, the household, childbirth, entertainment (m)

Geb.................................. the earth, fertility (m)

Hathor..............................cows, motherhood, love, childbirth, music, the stars, peace (f)

Horus ..............................solar energy, leadership, the Pharoahs (m)

Isis....................................motherhood, life, handicraft skills, lunar energy, magick skills (f)

Ma'at......judgment of the dead, logic, truth, honesty, balance (f)

Nephthys......dark magick, the night, mystery, dreams (f)

Nut......the sky, stars (f)

Osiris......agriculture, grains, civilization, religion, the underworld, rebirth (m)

Ra......the Sun, creation, rebirth, destiny, justice (m)

Sekhmet......destruction, war, protection (f)

Set...... conflict, anger, war, storms (m)

Thoth......knowledge, records, astronomy, mathematics, writing, spirituality, hidden wisdom (m)


## *Greek*

Aphrodite......love, romance, rebirth, relationships, female energy (f)

Apollo......the Sun, music, legal matters, philosophy, poetry, knowledge (m)

Ares......conflict, aggression, war (m)

Artemis............................ purity, childbirth, hunting, wild animals, the moon (f)

Athena...............................protection, strength, independence, handicraft skills, wisdom, architecture, warfare (f)

Bacchus.............................celebrations, wine, sexuality, theatrical arts (m)

Demeter.............................the harvest, agriculture, motherhood, family, civilization, magickal arts (f)

Hades................................the underworld, wealth (m)

Hecate...............................dark mysteries, crossroads, childbirth, the dead (f)

Hephaestus........................skill, craftsmen, fire, industry, productivity (m)

Hera..................................motherhood, marriage, the household, infidelities, beauty, luxury (f)

Hermes..............................messages, communication, medicine, astronomy, music, travel, literature (m)

Hestia................................ home and hearth (f)

Poseidon............................the oceans, earthquakes, horses, storms (m)

Zeus..................................weather, leadership, power, lightning (m)

## *Celtic*

Arianrhod........................motherhood, the heavens, fate, fertility (f)

Belenus.............................the sun, fertility, livestock, medicine, the arts (m)

Blodeuwedd.....................the maiden, beauty, youth, lunar energy, new beginnings, wisdom (f)

Brigid...............................the arts, divination, livestock, medicine, smithcraft and other arts (f)

Caillech............................crone, mysteries (f)

Cernunnos........................wildlife, fertility, abundance, the Horned One (m)

Cerridwen......................... wisdom, divination, the underworld, changes, rebirth (f)

Dadga...............................warriors, fatherhood, knowledge, life and death (m)

Danu.................................cattle, fertility, motherhood, cycles (f)

Epona...............................horses, wealth, livestock, nightmares (f)

Gofannon.........................all forms of skill and craft (m)

Lugh...................................the sun, skills and crafts, healing, music, warriors (m)

Morrigan............................battle, darkness, the crone, magickal arts (f)

Rhiannon...........................the moon, livestock, horses (f)


## *Norse*

Baldur................................goodness, honesty, forgiveness, integrity (m)

Bragi..................................literature, wit, speaking, poetry, music, creative inspiration (m)

Freya..................................love, sensuality, the moon, wealth, good luck, cats (f)

Freyr..................................abundance, sailors, bravery, fertility (m)

Frigga................................female energy, motherhood, marriage, handicrafts, destiny (f)

Hel.....................................the underworld, magickal arts, divination, crossroads (f)

Loki....................................trickster, stealth, revenge, dishonesty, disasters (m)

Odin.................................civilization, law, order, justice, knowledge, wisdom (m)

Thor.................................thunder, courage, battle (m)


## Roman

Roman Gods and Goddesses are a bit of a special case because they are really just renamed versions of the Greek Gods that came before them. So, just take note of the alternate names and see what they represent in the Greek section above.

Apollo..............................Apollo

Ceres................................Demeter

Diana...............................Artemis

Dionysis...........................Bacchus

Hecate..............................Hecate

Juno.................................Hera

Jupiter..............................Zeus

Mars................................Ares

Mercury...........................Hermes

Minerva...........................Athena

Neptune............................Poseidon

Pluto...................................Hades

Venus.................................Aphrodite

Vulcan...............................Hephaestus

# Section 2

## Purposes, Intentions and Goals

This is the section organized by your spell purpose or intention. When you have an idea for a spell, this is where you look to find all the various things that would give you the proper energy for that purpose.

# *Love*

Of all the purposes behind spellwork, I think it is safe to say
that this is the most common. Who doesn't want to find more
love in their lives? Well, I won't lecture on the issues of casting
love spells on unsuspecting potential partners and the potential
pitfalls of manufactured love. The fact is that love spells can be
done without infringing on anyone's free will so don't feel that
all love magick is the same.

This is a list for love spells, but if you are looking specifically
for sex, physical love or passion, check on the next chapter.
Many ingredients and correspondences are the same, but some
things are really only good for one but not the other.

### Herbs & Plants

Adam & Eve root, apple, avocado, Balm of Gilead, bedstraw,
black cohosh, bloodroot, brazil nuts, cardamom, catnip,
chamomile, cherry, chestnut, cinquefoil, cloves, clover,
coltsfoot, coriander, daffodil, damiana, dragon's blood,
elecampane, elm, evening primrose, fig, gardenia, geranium,
henbane, honeysuckle, hyacinth, ivy, jasmine, juniper, lavender,
lemon, lemon balm, lemon verbena, licorice, mandrake, maple,
meadowsweet, mimosa, myrtle, orchid, orris root, parsley,
plumeria, poppy, rose, saffron, snakeroot, St. John's Wort,
thyme, tonka beans, valerian, vanilla, vervain, willow, yarrow,
yerba mate, ylang-ylang,

**Stones**...................coral, emerald, garnet, lapis lazuli, pearl, red jasper, rose quartz, ruby

**Deities**.................. Hathor, Aphrodite, Freya, Bast

**Colors**...................red, pink, white

**Day**.......................Friday

**Planets**.................Venus, Mars

**Elements**.............Water

**Direction**.............South

# *Passion*

While passion often goes hand in hand with love, you can't really presume that the two are the same concept. They certainly aren't, especially when it comes to magick.

These are the supplies and ingredients you'll need when working with just physical love or sexuality. It may pertain to existing romantic relationships or not.

### Herbs & Plants

Adam & Eve root, avocado, caraway, cardamom, cinnamon, cloves, damiana, dill, garlic, ginger, ginseng, gum mastic, hibiscus, hickory, jasmine, lemongrass, licorice, nettle, orris root, patchouli, rosemary, saffron, savory, snakeroot, tuberose, vanilla, yerba mate, ylang-ylang

**Stones**..........................red jasper, garnet

**Deities**.........................Bast, Aphrodite, Freya

**Colors**..........................red

**Day**..............................Friday

**Planets**........................Venus, Mars

**Elements**....................Water, Fire

**Direction**....................South

# *Money*

Money can be a tricky subject when it comes to working spells, as some will immediately say that this is a forbidden area because we are not supposed to use magick for personal gain. Well, I think that is up for debate. I certainly don't condone greed or the excessive seeking of money, but why not use these skills to improve your own life when you need a little assistance. Everything in moderation, right?

## Herbs & Plants

Acacia, allspice, almond, ash, banana, basil, benzoin, bergamot, borage, calamus, cashew, cedar, cinnamon, cinquefoil, comfrey, Devil's Shoestring, dill, fern, flax, galangal, ginger, goldenseal, grape, heliotrope, High John, Irish moss, Job's Tears, marjoram, nutmeg, oak, oakmoss, patchouli, pecan, pine, pomegranate, poppy, rice, rowan, sassafras, snakeroot, Tonka beans, vervain, wood aloe, woodruff

**Stones**.....................aventurine, bloodstone, garnet, jade, malachite, pyrite, ruby, tiger eye, diamond, lodestone

**Deities**...................Hephaestus, Cernunnos, Freya

**Colors**....................green, orange, brown, gold

**Day**.........................Thursday

**Planets**..................Jupiter, the sun

**Elements**...............Earth

# *Protection*

Being able to protect yourself from physical threats as well as
psychic or magickal ones is important to many people. This
does mean a rather broad range of topics that can include
protection in general as well as other types of banishings. But
to keep things straight, I have another section for banishing
correspondences. This section is *just* for protection.

Be realistic in your safety assessments too. Don't attribute
every moment of bad luck as proof that someone has hexed
you, or that a spirit is out to get you.

And another warning, never ever rely solely on magick for
physical protection. I don't care how many spells you cast,
make sure you lock your door at night. The right spell can help
you get rid of an annoying person in your life, but a real stalker
should be handled by the police.

### Herbs & Plants

Acacia, acorn, agrimony, aloe, amaranth, angelica, anise,
asafoetida, ash, Balm of Gilead, barley, bay, bittersweet, birch,
blessed thistle, blueberry, burdock, calendula, caraway,
chrysanthemum, cinquefoil, cloves, clover, coriander, cumin,
curry, cypress, dill, eucalyptus, fennel, feverfew, foxglove,
garlic, hazel, heather, holly, horehound, Irish moss, larkspur,
lilac, lily, lime, lotus, mandrake, marjoram, mimosa, mistletoe,
mugwort, mullein, nettle, nutmeg, oak, Orris root, pennyroyal,
pepper, plantain, purslane, rue, sage, Solomon's Seal, star anise,
St. John's Wort, thyme, valerian, vetivert, violet, witch hazel,

wood aloe,

**Stones**........................amber, chalcedony, coral, hematite, jet, obsidian, onyx, peridot, turquoise

**Deities**...................... Bast, Bes, Sekhmet, Athena, Hestia

**Colors**........................Black, white, silver

**Day**............................Saturday

**Planets**......................Mars, Saturn,

**Elements**..................Earth

# *Banishing*

The section on protection is for all sorts of general protection purposes, but this is specifically for banishing. That can be banishing people from your lives but also spirits and simple negative energy.

## Herbs & Plants

Agrimony, angelica, asafoetida, basil, birch, buckthorn, cayenne, cloves, cumin, curry, dragon's blood, elder, elecampane, frankincense, galangal, garlic, heliotrope, horehound, hyssop, ivy, juniper, mandrake, mint, mistletoe, morning glory, mullein, nettle, nutmeg, pepper, pine, poke root, rose geranium, rosemary, rowan, rue, sandalwood, Solomon's Seal, star anise, tansy, vetivert, white sage, wormwood, yarrow

**Stones**.......................... Kunzite, onyx, topaz, tourmaline

**Deities**........................ *none in particular*

**Colors**.......................... Black

**Day**.............................. Saturday, Monday

**Planets**....................... Saturn

**Elements**.................. Earth

# *Health*

Healing magick and health spells can be powerful assets in combating illness or disease. They certainly can't replace true medical care, so never avoid going to the doctor in favor of a little spellwork.

Remember these are *magickal* correspondences, not medical ones. These herbs aren't to be used as medicinal ingredients.

### Herbs & Plants

Adder's Tongue, almond, aloe, angelica, Balm of Gilead, betony, bittersweet, camphor, carnation, coriander, cowslip, cypress, elder, eucalyptus, fennel, fern, feverfew, gardenia, garlic, geranium, goldenseal, honeysuckle, juniper, lime, maple, mint, mistletoe, myrrh, pine, plantain, plum, rose, rosemary, rue, saffron, sandalwood, sassafras, St. John's Wort, tansy, tobacco, willow.

**Stones**......................... Amazonite, hematite, jade, rose quartz, sugalite

**Deities**........................ Anubis, Hermes, Belenus

**Colors**......................... Blue, purple

**Day**.............................. Sunday

**Planets**....................... Sun

**Elements**................... Water

# Purification

Purification spells are used whenever you need to cleanse something, be it an altar tool, a place or even your own person. Things pick up energy all the time and should be purified periodically, even if they aren't physically dirty in any way.

If you are looking to get rid of active energy in your surroundings, try the banishing section.

### Herbs & Plants

Anise, bay, benzoin, betony, birch, bloodroot, cayenne, cedar, copal, fennel, frankincense, hemlock, henbane, hyssop, iris, juniper, lemon, lemon verbena, mimosa, myrrh, orange, parsley, pepper, rosemary, sandalwood, thyme, tobacco, turmeric, white sage, wood aloe, wolfsbane

**Stones**..........................Amber, calcite, salt

**Deities**........................ *none in particular*

**Colors**.......................... White, pink,

**Day**............................... Monday

**Planets**........................ *none in particular*

**Elements**.................. Fire

# Astral Travel and Psychic Abilities

These are the elements and items you need to help bring out your natural psychic skills, particularly with regards to exploring the astral.

Items that help with divination have also been included here since they are fundamentally doing the same thing, honing your natural psychic skills. If you really need to differentiate between divination or astral skills, you can check the other sections (like the herbs or stones) to see the specifics.

Another section later on will cover sleep and dreams, which may also be of interest.

### Herbs & Plants

Acacia, adder's tongue, alder, angelica, anise, bay, beech, belladonna, benzoin, borage, broom, calendula, camphor, cherry, chervil, cinnamon, coltsfoot, dandelion, elecampane, eyebright, fig, flax, galangal, grape, gum mastic, hazel, heliotrope, honeysuckle, lemon balm, lemongrass, lilac, lovage, mace, marigold, mugwort, pumpkin, rose, rowan, rue, savory, star anise, St. John's Wort, sweetgrass, vanilla, willow, wormwood, yarrow

### Stones

Amethyst, aquamarine, azurite, beryl, carnelian, celestite, emerald, lapis lazuli, moldavite, moonstone, peridot, sugalite, turquoise

**Deities**........................ Isis, Cerridwen, Morrigan, Hel

**Colors**......................... Purple, silver

**Day**............................. Monday, Wednesday

**Planets**....................... Mercury, the Moon, Pluto

**Elements**.................. Air, water

# *Sleep and Dreams*

A little magick can help you sleep easier and better, and can help you get free of nightmares. Whether you are looking for a more restful sleep or just want to encourage better dreaming, these are the supplies you will need.

As I've said many times already, these are generally not medicinal items (particularly the herbs) so use them in a magickal manner only. The exception would be with chamomile or valerian. They make excellent sleep-inducing teas that actually work on a physical level.

### Herbs & Plants

Agrimony, betony, chamomile, cinquefoil, elder, hibiscus, holly, hops, jasmine, lavender, lovage, marjoram, mimosa, mullein, poppy, purslane, thyme, valerian, vervain, violet

**Stones**......................... Amethyst, azurite, celestite, chalcedony, citrine, coral, garnet, peridot, red jasper, topaz

**Deities**........................ Nephthys

**Colors**......................... Purple, white

**Day**.............................. Monday

**Planets**....................... Moon, Neptune

**Elements**.................... Air, Water

# *Creativity*

Looking to magick for a little creative muse is an excellent way to help your mind grow into some new ideas. Traditionally speaking, it's not as common a purpose for spell work so you won't find as many correspondences here as you do in other sections.

For the Deities, I've taken a little more liberty than usual since few Gods really rule over this trait specifically. These are Gods and Goddesses who are involved in many types of artistic areas or who are patrons to various crafts.

### Herbs & Plants

Beech, caraway, carnation, cinnamon, grape, eyebright, honeysuckle, mace, mint, mistletoe, rowan, savory, vervain

**Stones**..........................amazonite, amethyst, citrine, fluorite

**Deities**.........................Isis, Bast, Hermes, Gofannon, Hephaestus, Brigid, Bragi,

**Colors**..........................Blue, yellow, purple, silver

**Day**..............................Wednesday

**Planets**........................Mercury, Neptune

**Elements**...................Water

# *Confidence*

Having good self-esteem and being confident in yourself is a valuable asset in any part of your life. You can use a little magick to help boost your confidence, which may improve all other parts of your life at the same time. These types of spells can work well if you are after love or money, rather than the traditional types of spells. When its confidence you lack, work on that directly.

Items that help bring your courage and strength have been added in here as well.

### Herbs & Plants

Allspice, black cohosh, borage, carnation, fennel, ginger, mullein, oakmoss, pennyroyal, platain, poke root, thyme, tobacco, vanilla,

**Stones**..........................Amazonite, bloodstone, garnet, obsidian, pearl, peridot, rhodonite, ruby, sodalite

**Deities**........................ Athena, Horus, Lugh, the Dagda, Thor

**Colors**.......................... Yellow

**Day**.............................. Sunday

**Planets**.......................Sun

**Elements**................... Fire

# *Spirituality*

Yes, this section is a little vague but if you are seeking spirituality then you likely know what I'm talking about. These are the materials and correspondences that are involved with generally seeking the Divine, regardless of your specific beliefs or faith. Any of these things will open up your heart and mind to get in touch with larger forces outside of ourselves.

### Herbs & Plants

Chervil, cinnamon, frankincense, gardenia, myrrh, sandalwood, walnut

**Stones**.......................... Amber, jet, lapis lazuli, moldavite, sapphire, sugalite,

**Deities**......................... *none in particular*

**Colors**.......................... Purple, gold, silver, blue, white

**Day**............................... Monday

**Planets**........................ Moon, Pluto

**Elements**.................... Air, Water

# *Fertility*

Though we already have a section on health correspondences, this section is specifically for fertility and trying to get pregnant. This has been a long-standing purpose for doing magick.

Just remember that these are presented as magickal components rather than medicinal ones. Please never take any of these herbs without clearing it with your doctor. And speaking of doctors, remember that most infertility has some sort of physical cause so exhaust your medical options while still trying some magick. Just don't rely on spells alone.

### Herbs & Plants

Apple, banana, black cohosh, cardamom, daffodil, fig, geranium, grape, hawthorn, ivy, lily, mandrake, mistletoe, myrtle, oak, olive, parsley, patchouli, pine, poppy, rice

**Stones**........................ Aventurine, garnet, pearl

**Deities**....................... Bast, Geb, Hathor, Isis, Artemis, Aphrodite, Demeter, Hera, Arianrhod, Danu, Freyr, Frigga,

**Colors**........................ Green, brown

**Day**............................. Monday, Friday

**Planets**....................... Venus, Moon

**Elements**................... Water, Earth

# More Purposes

This is a bit of a miscellaneous section, with additional spell intentions that are less common and have fewer correspondences than the others. But I figured that they were important enough to get a little mention anyway.

## Safe Travel

**Herbs & Plants**: Comfrey, feverfew, lucky hand, mint, wormwood

**Stones**: Chalcedony, coral, jade, sodalite, topaz

**Colors**: Yellow

**Element:** Air

## Weather Magick

**Herbs & Plants**: Broom, fern, heather,

**Stones:** *none in particular*

**Colors**: Blue

**Element:** Water

## Communication

**Herbs & Plants**: Aspen, hickory

**Stones:** Emerald, kunzite, kyanite, labradorite, pyrite, sodalite

**Colors**: Yellow

**Element:** Air


## Fidelity

**Herbs & Plants**: Licorice, lily, magnolia, scullcap, yerba mate, olive,

**Stones:** Diamond, malachite, rose quartz, turquoise

**Colors**: White, pink

**Element:** Water


## Legal Matters

**Herbs & Plants**: Buckthorn, calendula, comfrey, galangal, marigold, hickory

**Stones:** *none in particular*

**Colors**: Orange

**Element:** Earth

# SABBATS

This section is all about the 8 sacred days of the year, known as the Sabbats. Not all Pagan paths acknowledge these, so I apologize if these don't apply. But so many diverse believes celebrate this version of the Wheel of the Year, I figured it needed to be added.

A mix of correspondences have been included with each holiday, and are used in celebration of the day rather than in a purposeful spell like the other sections of this book. This is a brief snapshot of each Sabbat since this isn't really about spellwork. There are some great books out there just on these holidays so you can do further research if you want.

And in case you are not familiar with the solstices and equinoxes, the dates vary because they are based on astrological events that don't happen at exactly the same time each year.

Use these correspondences to decorate your altar or even the whole house, and to start up traditions that are common to each holiday. Getting in tune with the cycles of the year is a great way to build up your own inner magick.

## *Yule*

**Other names**: Saturnalia, winter solstice, Alban Arthuan

**Date**: December 20th, 21st or 22nd

**Meaning**: The longest night of the year, which means the days will start to slowly lengthen after this day. So Yule celebrates the return of the sun and the start of the light half of the year. It is a holiday of rebirth and beginnings. In the mythic cycle, this is when the God is born.

**Activities**:  Decorating an indoor tree, giving gifts, lighting a Yule log, visiting friends and family, kissing under mistletoe

**Herbs**: Pine, holly, cinnamon, myrrh, frankincense, bayberry, ivy, mistletoe

**Foods**: Nuts, dried fruit, mulled wine, turkey, pork, apples, pears

**Colors**: Silver, white, red, green


## *Imbolc*

**Other names**: Candlemas, Brigid's Day, Oimelc, Festival of Light, Lupercalia

**Date**: February 2nd

**Meaning**: The very first signs of spring are starting to appear and Imbolc marks the time of year when livestock would be giving their first milk of the year. The Celtic Goddess Brigid was particularly honored on this day.

**Activities**: Lighting bonfires or candles, spring cleaning, starting new seeds, telling stories

**Herbs**: Chamomile, carnation, rosemary, clover, heather, buttercup,

**Foods**: Fresh milk, raisins, honey, sunflower seeds, sesame seeds

**Colors**: Pink, yellow, lavender, white

## *Ostara*

**Other names**: Spring equinox, Lady Day, Alban Eiler, Bacchanalia

**Date**: March 20th, 21st or 22nd

**Meaning**: Another celebration of spring, more focusing on the new life that is seen around us. Baby animals are a big theme at this time of the year, as are flowers and eggs.

**Activities**: Coloring eggs, decorating with flowers, bird watching

**Herbs**: Jasmine, daffodil, any new wildflowers

**Foods**: Eggs, maple syrup, hot cross buns, honey, fish

**Colors**: Light green, pale blue, pink, lavender

## *Beltane*

**Other names**: May Day, Walpurgis Night, Rudemas, Whitsun, Lady Day (yes, same as Ostara)

**Date**: May 1st

**Meaning**:  Seasons have shifted from spring into summer and the fertility of the year is celebrated. Growth and development are major themes at Beltane, as is sexuality and fertility. The God is now grown to a man and he consummates the sacred marriage with the Goddess.

**Activities**:  Dancing the maypole, lighting bonfires, gathering wildflowers, sporting games, dancing, handfastings

**Herbs**: Rose, lilac, vanilla, angelica, hawthorn, primrose, lilac, yarrow

**Foods**: Dairy, honey, oats, salad greens, wine

**Colors**: Red, white, dark green, blue

## Litha

**Other names**: Summer solstice, Midsummer, St. John's Eve, Feast of Epona, Vestalia, Alban Heruin

**Date**: June 20th, 21st or 22nd

**Meaning**: Summer is at its peak, and the days begin to darken after this day. The Goddess is in her Mother phase, and the earth is filled with growing abundance.

**Activities**: Herb harvesting, fairy magick, dowsing, singing, blessing the crops

**Herbs**: Vervain, honeysuckle, nettle, rose, chamomile, fern, rue, wisteria, St. John's Wort

**Foods**: Citrus fruits, carrots, mead, any fresh vegetables

**Colors**: Green, gold, yellow, red


## Lammas

**Other names**: Lughnsadh, Thingtide, Harvest Home

**Date**: August 1st

**Meaning**: This is the first of 3 festivals to mark the harvests of the year. Grains were harvested at this time, and they make the central focus for celebrations. This was the time of sacrifice for a successful harvest.

**Activities**: Baking bread, making corn husk dolls, games and competitions, making flower crowns

**Herbs**: Sandalwood, ginseng, frankincense, sunflower, oak, cyclamen

**Foods**: Grains, corn, summer squash, potatoes, acorns, apples, berries, grapes

**Colors**: Brown, gold, bronze, yellow, orange

## *Mabon*

**Other names**: Fall or autumn equinox, Cornucopia, Alban Elfed,

**Date**: September 20th, 21st or 22nd

**Meaning**: Winter is making itself known as fall settles in, and Mabon marks the second harvest celebration. Helping and sharing are big themes for this Sabbat, which is likely the origins of modern Thanksgiving.

**Activities**: Giving to charity, making wine, hiking, fishing

**Herbs**: Cedar

**Foods**: Grapes, blackberries apples, pomegranates, beans, corn

**Colors**: Gold, scarlet, purple, deep green

## *Samhain*

**Other names**: Halloween, All Saints Day, Feast of All Souls

**Date**: October 31st

**Meaning**: This is the one Pagan Sabbat that is known throughout the mainstream world, though many aren't clear on its true meaning. The day marks the final harvest and the final portion of the dark half of the year. The veil between this world and the next is thin, and contact with the spirit world is much easier than any other time. The God that was born at Yule has died, and the Goddess mourns his death with the coming of winter.

**Activities**: Divination, honoring the dead or ancestors, carving Jack o'lanterns,

**Herbs**: Sage, mugwort, wormwood, comfrey, mandrake, dragon's blood, thistle, oak, patchouli

**Foods**: Pumpkins, apples, cider, pomegranate, corn, hazelnuts

**Colors**: black and orange

# PUTTING A SPELL TOGETHER

Finally, you might want a few tips on how to put all of this together to make a new spell of your own. Unfortunately, that's is supposed to be up to you. That's the whole point here. I can give you a couple of pointers, but that's all. Your own creative energies are what make a spell powerful, not me giving you step-by-step instructions.

Firstly, decide on your purpose. Be specific and take some time to figure out what you want to accomplish. Don't rely on useless ideas like "good luck". Nobody just wants luck. You want something in particular, so go after that. Then read through this guide and see what kinds of supplies and other factors will play into your purpose.

The tricky part is knowing how to work them together. But that's also the most fun part. Take stock of what you have access to first, since there is no point building a spell around ingredients you don't have. Then think about how you want to proceed.

Stones can be carried with you or arranged on an altar, herbs can be stuffed into bags for talismans, and you can add color through candles, ribbons, cloth or flowers. Time your spells for a certain day or when a planet is in a certain point in the sky. Have your altar face a certain direction during your ritual, or have images of animals within your spell materials. Anoint candles with certain essential oils, or burn herbs as incense. Tie knots in colored yarn, drink tea made with herbs, burn messages on bits of paper or any other action that blends these components together.

You see, there are an almost endless list of ways you can mix and match these elements to create a spell. So now's the time to get creative and make your own magick.

# *Sources and References*

Scott Cunningham, "The Complete Book of Incense, Oils and Brews", Llewellyn Publications, USA, 1997

Edain McCoy, "Sabbats: A Witch's Approach to Living the Old Ways", Llewellyn Publications, USA, 2001

Judika Illes, "Pure Magic", Weiser Books, USA, 2001

Deborah Lipp, "The Way of Four", Llewellyn Publications, USA, 2004

Free Witchcraft Spells < http://www.free-witchcraft-spells.com > 2014

www.ingramcontent.com/pod-product-compliance
Lightning Source LLC
Chambersburg PA
CBHW070642030426
42337CB00020B/4128